Happy Spouse, Happy House

Melvin Finney

FINNEYBOOKS

ISBN: 978-1-948581-80-6

Editor: Sharp Editorial, LLC

Lincross Publishing

Dedication

This book is dedicated to the Finney family. I love you all so much, especially my beautiful wife – you are an incredible woman, and I love you dearly.

To my pastors, Tye and Shante Tribbett, for being great examples to my wife and me and always being there for us.

This book is also dedicated to love – those in love and those fighting for love. May you find it, and may it keep you.

To the spouses trying their best to do the right thing, this book is for you. Your spouse sees you, and so does God.

FINNEYBOOKS

Acknowledgments

To the married couples we spend time with and talk to, thank you for being excellent role models and allowing my wife and me to learn from you.

To my editor, Laci Swann, thank you for giving a balanced perspective.

To my book cover artist, Desiree Murphy, thank you for your outstanding work.

Table of Contents

A Letter to the Reader……………………………………9

Introduction…………………………………………14

1. A Two-Way Street ……………………………..17
2. Communication ………………………………..32
3. Partnership……………………………………..42
4. The House of The Ring …………………………..50
5. Who Cares ………………………………………..57
6. Don't Change After the Ring ………………..65
7. Your Partner is NOT Your Sex Slave ……….73
8. Your Partner is NOT Your Bank Account ….82
9. Say Yes then Say No ………………………...89
10. Commitment ……………………………….....97
11. Walk in Love…………………………………105

A Letter to the Reader

My name is Melvin Finney, and I want to share my heart with you.

Growing up, life was hard, and my choices didn't make life any easier. I grew up breaking the law. I grew up doing things the wrong way on purpose. I knew right from wrong, but I chose wrong more often than not. Often, with age comes wisdom, and I'm grateful those years are behind me and that I now face the day with restored vision.

Since giving my life to Jesus Christ, I see life through a different set of lenses. I understand the many wonderful layers of love, growth, and relationships, and I see new and better ways to love and be loved by your spouse. With Jesus in my heart, my relationships have become more profound, and I've developed a stronger understanding of my identity, values, and purpose.

I've been married for over 14 years. I married my high school sweetheart. It's been more than 20 years since we walked the halls of our high school, and my wife and I have grown as individuals, as a couple, and as parents.

I talk to numerous men and women daily about their relationships and roles in their marriage. A lot of men and women tell me their concerns about their spouse and marriage, and not only am I grateful for their trust in my wisdom, but I am thankful for their honesty because their insight and experiences paved the way for this book. This book is reflective of the many conversations I've had with family and close friends, people who believe there is an unbalance in their marriage. They feel taken advantage of as if they're receiving the short end of the stick.

During a church sermon, I once learned that just because someone's feelings differ from yours does not make their perspective less real. We may not see eye-to-eye with our partner, but to acknowledge their feelings is an outward display of love and respect.

After reading this book, I would love for you to walk away with something to help your marriage flourish.

Although I'm a believer in love, I did not write this book to change the way the world looks at marriage. I wrote this book to give a different perspective on a topic that many fail to see, and that's the wants of their partner and, perhaps, a lack of support and communication.

Marriage is sacred and should be honored and respected, and among the many layers of marriage, equality, inclusion, and integrity are nested and should be revered. Equality is a must to achieve happiness in a marriage. Equality is a must in society, and that should be demonstrated in relationships, too. Each partner should also be welcomed in their spouse's everyday activities, not merely present but included, and integrity should be shared at its highest level. Your spouse depends on you to honor your word.

I'm not trying to leverage anyone to have the upper hand in their household. I'm encouraging equality and want to examine why we do certain things in a marriage. We often respond to miscommunication and challenges in marriage with temporary solutions that only seem to focus on the now but do nothing in the long run.

When a man makes a poor decision, why does he choose to buy his partner a gift so that she will forgive him?

On the flip side, when a woman does something she feels she should apologize for, why does she offer her man sex?

We need to unlearn the old way of doing things, and each household should create a new system based on their unique relationship, a system that promotes respect and consideration.

Often, inequality is rooted in miscommunication. Men are not listening to what women want, and women are not listening to what men want. People often blindly follow trends and try to keep up with the culture instead of cultivating a lifestyle that best fits their marriage.

Our marriages are worth more than allowing the blind to lead the blind. We need and deserve trusted pillars of wisdom and solid examples of healthy relationships. I hope to be a guide for men and a source of understanding for women. I hope to facilitate sound discussions, and here we are, about to dive into a book rooted in personal theories, feelings, and insight.

There's no time like the present to rewrite the narrative of what constitutes a healthy relationship, so let's begin!

Introduction

In a biblically traditional household, the man is considered the head of the household, yet we must remember that woman was made from man's rib. God used Adam's rib to form Eve. God demonstrated that Adam and Eve were made from the same substance, both bearing God's image and likeness (Genesis 1:27), and so women must be treasured and loved. Therefore, a sound marriage is a partnership in which everything should be discussed to determine the best outcomes and when both people care to make the other person feel respected and loved. If you want your marriage to not only survive but thrive, both parties must actively invest in their relationship.

Consider figuring out what to do for your partner to make their day special, and if this is not reciprocated, a partnership will not experience the joy it deserves and the love it committed to sharing. For example – if a woman wakes up and reminds her husband of all he has to accomplish that day because she cares about his goals, and then cooks his favorite breakfast to get his day started on the right foot, she is clearly going out of her way to make his day easier and special, but if he fails to reciprocate, there's an immediate imbalance. An imbalance can lead to false perceptions of love or lack of love, which can severely injure key elements of the relationship like communication, empathy, and trust. Unreciprocated love gives the enemy space to divide and conquer.

Although the wife did not perform acts of kindness merely to receive something in return, she ends up receiving the short end of the stick when her husband fails to balance her acts of love, and this is commonplace, unfortunately, in many marriages.

But why?

Why are we more inclined to take rather than give?

Healthy relationships travel a two-way street. Otherwise, they'll have a collision.

1

A Two-Way Street

Too many marriages are lopsided. One person often benefits more than the other, and that's not the type of partnership God intended for our lives. Ephesians 5:24-27 outlines that sentiment clearly:

Now as the church submits to Christ, so also wives should submit to their husbands in everything. Husbands, love your wives, just as Christ loved the church and gave himself up for her to make her holy, cleansing her by the washing with water through the word, and to present her to himself as a radiant church, without stain or wrinkle or any other blemish, but holy and blameless.

Marriage requires effect and thought, day in and day out. That seems like a lot of work, but the reality is, marriage *is* hard work, not grueling work as in torture or physical pain but continual, mindful effort. When both parties fail to continually nurture their relationship, and not only when it feels right or is convenient, the relationship falls to the wayside.

Life gets chaotic and busy, I know, but commit to starting your day off on the right foot for your partner. Maybe upon waking up, you discuss what your day looks like and how you can help one another. Maybe you discuss who's making breakfast or dinner plans that evening. Perhaps you eat breakfast together, or maybe you leave a note in your partner's lunch bag. A lot of times, we think marriages fail due to major occurrences like infidelity, when, in fact, failures are often small situations rooted in miscommunication – talking about the kids' schedules, chores around the house, and so forth. Each marriage's morning situation looks different from the next, but the point of the matter is, a successful morning is rooted in communication, selflessness, and a willingness to help one another. A little goes a long way.

In a healthy marriage, will someone have to occasionally sacrifice to help their partner?

Yes.

Sacrifice is one of the most important things to do to maintain a relationship. That's not to say the sacrifice should involve pain or suffering. Instead, this is about choosing your partner's joy or needs and helping them in ways they need or want. Your marriage is a garden, and gardens need perpetually watered, weeded, and fed. Otherwise, nothing will blossom but mangy weeds.

Men, we need to understand that ever since a woman was born, society has pushed her mindset toward getting married and having children, usually much earlier than men. Little girls often receive a baby doll as a Christmas present or birthday gift. When she gets older, she might receive a kitchen set or a fake vacuum cleaner. The baby doll comes equipped with diapers and food, encouraging young girls to change and feed the baby. The vacuum cleaner teaches them how to clean the floor, and the kitchen set has fake dishes and fake food, teaching them how to maintain a kitchen at an early age. These toys subconsciously prepare women to be married, take care of a household, and have kids. Of course, there are other toys for young girls to play with like a jump rope, board games, and art projects, but young girls are normally inundated with caretaker-like toys, grooming them to be a wife and mother.

On the opposite end of the table, in many households, boys are usually not taught to get married upon college graduation or around that age. Young boys are gifted fake guns, video games, construction tools, and fast cars, mostly toys to promote working with their hands, perhaps as to why men are work-driven at an early age.

Basically, society pushes its old western ways on each generation, and the outcomes are not conducive to healthy, equal partnerships.

Are some women more inclined to love the idea of marriage more than the marriage itself?

Are most men afraid of marriage because they feel like most of the "power" they cultivated growing up is now gone because they are subject to responsibility and accountability?

These are questions worth examining, especially in the context of your relationship.

A lot of my male role models were not faithful to their partners. I was always told to never be faithful to one woman. I was encouraged to have options and not settle down. Sadly, many adult male figures teach their young men to not settle for one woman or how to get away with never being faithful, and many of those men preaching that backward narrative grew up thinking that marriage is one-sided because they watched their uncle or dad bend over backward for Auntie or Mom, never seeing a woman treat a man with respect or honor their marriage. Older men tell younger men never to be faithful because they think life is geared to benefit women more because of what they've experienced, which leaves certain men feeling disgruntled and frustrated about the unbalance in their relationship.

In some marriages, the woman gets everything she wants from the moment she says, "I do." She receives the fancy proposal, expensive engagement ring, costly wedding band, beautiful dress, and extravagant honeymoon. When these grand gestures are unappreciated or taken for granted, men feel less inclined to want to be part of these major milestones, and thus, the narrative of imbalanced marriages continue, but the root of the cause is never addressed.

When marriage is the topic of discussion, and it veers into the subject of finances, many questions are often examined:

When two people fall in love, does that automatically mean one person is entitled to spend their partner's money?

Should two people split marriage costs down the middle?

How much is too much to spend on a wedding?

If the man does not pay for the wedding, does that mean he doesn't love his partner?

Is the man's reward the honeymoon?

After the grandeur wedding, months of festivities leading up to the big day, and the exchange of rings, it's not uncommon for men to wonder where they belong among this planning process and string of events, aside from paying for it. That's not to say men need or want something tangible in return. However, nothing really exists yet because society has a stronghold on the confines of man and woman's role leading up to marriage and within marriage.

The imbalances in relationships span across nearly every situation, down to gift-giving and household chores, and most situations are rooted in consumerism and the social media comparison trap. For a holiday like Valentine's Day, a man is frowned upon if he does not buy his wife lavish gifts, nice lingerie, or something worthy of showing off via social media, and with that same lingerie, a woman may feel as though sex should be her gift because of the gift her spouse bought. Is that to say sex is contingent on a holiday or present or that this should be the standard for how love and thoughtfulness are exchanged among a couple?

From holidays to regular ol' days of the week, equal treatment and support reap a happy house, a house that will withstand the trials of time and add value to the home because of the respect, love, and effort each person shares with their partner. From experience, partners are willing to go above and beyond for their loved one when they feel appreciated and their efforts are reciprocated, yet society has created traditions that formed relationship imbalances, and this impacts relationships for the worse.

There's a common narrative that encourages men to work demanding hours on the job, fix things around the home, and handle the laborious chores inside and outside of the house, and many men assume these responsibilities because that is what they're taught, told, and shown. That is not to say it's another generation's fault for the way young women regard men and their respective roles, yet this unbalance trickles down to children and teaches them to either not be self-sufficient or that certain gender roles are acceptable.

The more we stress equality and, more importantly, the more we practice equality, the better a relationship will be. If each person in a marriage concentrated on the other person in the marriage, there would be no lack. From a man's perspective, there are women who are taught to get certain things from men, treating the relationship like a transaction. I call this "The Dope Boy Effect." The Dope Boy Effect is when a woman thinks a man's job is to spoil them and do nice things for them without reciprocation. In the streets, a dope boy has a lot of money, so to spoil his girl is nothing, but he usually has several women in his life and isn't faithful to one of them. She doesn't have to do anything but look pretty. In a marriage, however, both parties need to give and receive what they want. This is not contingent on looks or gift-giving but the basis of love and respect in a partnership.

Let me be clear – there is nothing wrong with a man taking care of a woman if that's what he wants to do. Genuine actions and words from the heart create a bond and memories between two people and establish foundations of love, respect, and admiration. However, some women won't give a man a chance unless he can buy her nice things, and this has put a serious damper on the strength and existence of genuine, long-standing relationships. In addition to the existence of fewer relationships and the abundance of imbalanced relationships, could it be that some men are trying to teach their young men not to endure the unbalance they endured throughout their former or current partnership?

As partners, men and women alike, we need to practice productive communication. Men, if you're uncomfortable about the patterns and expectations within your partnership, or about being in an unbalanced situation, commit to not talking about your partner behind her back. Instead, assume a leadership role and encourage a healthy conversation. Remember, there's more than one way to arrive at a destination. If one person in a marriage always gets their way, whether that's the man or the women, that's a clear indication that someone's needs at not being met. In a healthy relationship, a two-way street must be traveled for everyone to be happy and to avoid an awful collision. A solid relationship is contingent on this, and this is a lesson we lack in disseminating.

Some people teach others out of hurt, and this also perpetuates unhealthy standards for future generations. For example – A woman in an abusive relationship is now divorced and telling her niece not to make her husband a dinner plate, something her niece never minded doing, as this was a thoughtful way to show her partner love after his long day at work. This woman is hurting, angry, and has yet to deal with her trauma, but as she speaks to her niece and other girlfriends, she unknowingly gives negative relationship advice. On the other hand, examine the man who was in a toxic relationship that ended due to infidelity. Now, he tells his friends to avoid commitment because women shouldn't be trusted. Between the abused woman and wronged man, their bad advice is now affecting other relationships. In those situations, I don't believe the man or woman is trying to destroy their loved ones' relationships; however, both were hurt, have yet to heal, and are now speaking their truth, which is rooted in pain.

Question – Has your pain from the past stopped the flow of appreciation for your partner?

If so, it is imperative that you deal with the pain.

As human beings, we must collectively teach our next generation to love and support their partner. More importantly, before you teach someone else, you must understand that your partner is equally important, and the way you feel about yourself and how you want to be treated is the way you should treat your partner.

Commit to learning your partner.

Discover their love language.

Learn their expectations of you and how they want to be loved.

Once you uncover those layers, you will have a better understanding of what your partner wants for themselves and what they want for you.

Why be in a relationship with someone and not treat them with the love and respect you desire for yourself?

Refuse to follow the cultural wave that promotes using people rather than loving people. Refuse to hold your relationship to the gender-specific standards society deems appropriate.

Women are still commonly regarded as a maid in the household. This construct is horribly wrong and needs to be changed. Everything is to be shared and divided between husband and wife. That's the only way you can truly understand how your partner feels when they're explaining something to you because you did it before and you know how it feels to not want to do something or particularly like a certain chore. You will have more compassion and understanding to support any decision made by your partner after you've walked a mile in their shoes.

A woman's job is not only to keep the house clean.

A man's job is not only to pay the bills.

You are partners, and as partners, you commit to creating a fair, loving household.

Treat other people how you want to be treated.

Love your partner how you want to be loved.

Make yourself available when your partner needs you the most, and you will know when that is by communication and time spent learning one another. It's impossible for one person in a partnership to understand the value of an equal partnership if the other person does not care or seek to understand the importance of a two-way street. You will be fighting an uphill battle with no victory in sight. Although the keys to a successful relationship involve communication and fairness, many couples tend to stay in unbalanced situations for several reasons, such as children and financial security.

The unbalance often comes from a mask someone wore when first meeting – you know, during the "Honeymoon Phase." You may have liked a lot of things about this new person but ignored the qualities you didn't care too much for, and now those initial annoyances have grown into a full-fledged monster. Some people hold back the worst things about themselves because they're trying to change, or they know that most people won't tolerate their behavior. So, they hide it hoping that it won't come out eventually. When you do that, you are essentially taking your partner's choice from them. This is damaging because by hiding your true self, you never give your partner a full chance and opportunity to decide to love you based upon all information. However, the detriment to the person who hides the unhealthy behavior to find love is that by not showing all of yourself, you will never be confident in love within that relationship. Honesty is important at every stage, especially from the beginning.

Many feel that equality equates to or feels like a loss as if someone standing beside you and not behind you means you're no longer winning or capable of winning. Ladies and fellas, you don't lose anything by encouraging your partner to be your equal. In fact, you gain a life partner.

"If a house be divided against itself, that house cannot stand."

(Mark 3:25)

2

Communication

Communication is an important key in any relationship, whether personal, professional, or romantic. The more your partner knows about what you want, the better they can understand you and accommodate your needs because communication breeds accountability. When you fully express your wants and desires to your partner and your partner listens with an open heart, then both parties are in the position to be respectful and compliant with the information exchanged.

For example: When you go to a restaurant, the host typically asks how many people will be dining. After you've been seated, your waiter greets you and asks what you'd like to drink and eat. Following your meal, you're then asked what you'd like for dessert. Because of the ongoing, clear communication between you and your server, your needs and wants are covered, and the only thing you need to focus on is enjoying yourself. Basically, you got exactly what you wanted. Well, this analogy is similar to the way you're supposed to communicate in a partnership. No, your partner is not your server, but you should be open to where they know everything they need to know about you because it's communicated directly and kindly, and they now have the information to better love and assist you. Relationships are supposed to facilitate a continual, open line of communication because people are always changing, growing, and learning, so it's always important to talk to your partner.

Men, you don't lose by telling your partner what is sexually attractive to you, but you will lose if you look elsewhere because you don't give your partner a chance to learn and satisfy those needs. Worse, you lose their trust when you go elsewhere, and that often creates irreparable damage. Women, you don't lose by telling your partner what type of style or swag you want your man to have, what turns you on in the bedroom, and what interests you in life. You only gain when choosing to communicate. When you give your partner a chance to learn what makes you tick, you won't look outside of your partnership because you are opting to communicate first.

Ladies, picture this – it's your birthday week and all your friends at work keep telling you about this new trend that all the men are doing for their wives for their birthday – a staycation at a beautiful hotel and spa. Later that evening, your husband asks you what you want to do for your birthday. You smile and let him know that anything he chooses is fine. Normally, your husband is up on all of the latest trends and never misses a beat, but now you're getting older, he's up for a promotion at work, and he asks you what you want to do because he knows he's been bombarded by work commitments. Your birthday rolls around and he gives you your morning birthday breakfast before you both go to work. At work, all of your girlfriends are asking about your man's plans for the night, and you're confident he has something amazing planned because he's always on point, not thinking that he asked you because he's been preoccupied trying to better your future with his promotion. Well, when you arrive home, you see that your husband hired a personal chef to make your favorite meal and invited your parents and a friend from work. The house looks amazing, and as the guests arrive, they're smiling from ear to ear because of the nice dinner and thoughtful gesture. Throughout the night, everyone is shooting you the girl-you-chose-the-right-husband look, but the friend from work is giving you the petty eye as if to say she knows you're feeling some type of way because you thought your husband would've planned a staycation. Even though the husband's gesture was generous and thoughtful, a private chef is not what she wanted. At this point, you have two choices – enjoy your night and ignore your guest's petty stares or act out and let everyone know how unpleased you are with your birthday dinner. Communication would've made the night better because your husband could've saved his time and money by planning a staycation, the gift you really wanted. After all, he wanted to make you happy, and your thoughts mattered to him regarding your special day. Communication goes a long way in every situation. One partner's expectations lead to the other partner's unappreciated efforts.

Sure, communication changes the face of every relationship, but I am not naïve – I know that communication is not always an easy feat. Imagine how much smoother relationships would be if we said exactly how we felt, but when our loved one's feelings are involved, we often fear that some conversations may hurt or offend, so we steer clear, hold our emotions inside, and the turmoil eventually rears its ugly head. Some may need to speak to a professional to learn how to better express themselves, or maybe they need a spiritual breakthrough to find their voice, even in minor situations. If you are not dealing with any serious problems that will prevent you from speaking to your partner, then you need to prioritize opening up and communicating because your relationship depends on it.

Equally as important as communication is honesty. Being honest is a must. Plus, keeping a lie going is hard because you must remember every lie you've spoken. Just tell the truth the first time and you won't have to worry or keep track. Allow your partner to feel safe to agree or disagree with whatever you present. Don't keep secrets from your partner, thinking you're saving them from finding out something about you or that they might look at you differently. Perhaps your last relationship didn't work because you had commitment issues, or maybe you're afraid to get hurt. Those hot topics need to be discussed, not necessarily the day you meet, but before you say, "I do."

If your partner hurt you and it still bothers you to your core, don't hold in these feelings and don't lie and say you forgive them.

Communicate!

Say something.

Don't blow up over little things because of misplaced anger, and don't stop wanting to do nice things for your partner because you're still upset about your argument. If you begin doing this, you risk creating a pattern for how you deal with your emotions. Then, resentment will be your go-to. Resentment can quickly become the new normal in your relationship, and eventually, you won't be able to stand each other because of a lack of communication. Encourage healthy communication. Expressing your concerns is not an invitation to have destructive dialogue that does more harm than good.

Keep it real with your partner.

Imagine this – you're happily in a relationship. You and your partner plan a special day out, no kids. The day finally arrives. Your bags are packaged, the car has a full tank, and the babysitter is at your front door. Well, what if your partner no longer feels like going on the trip? What if they'd rather stay in with you instead of venturing out for the night? Should they bite their tongue and go, or would you be happy that they told you exactly how they felt instead of letting you waste your time and money on something they no longer wanted to do? After all, it could always get rescheduled for another day or you could find something fun to do other than what was planned. People change their minds all the time. That is why it's important to communicate and stay up to date with your partner's feelings because if you don't, your relationship will suffer and wither, and someone else may try to step in, too. No one should know your partner better than you. It's your responsibility to make time for your partner and their inner-most feelings.

When your partner is talking to you, are you listening to respond, or do you listen to understand?

When your partner talks to you, is your goal to win the conversation or gain understanding?

If your goal is to win, you might risk lying, raising your voice, or becoming upset if the conversation doesn't go your way, but if your goal is to understand your partner, your approach will be rooted in love and respect. Be slow to speak and quick to listen (James 1:19). You don't need to have an answer ready after every sentence. Your number one goal is to evaluate the situation and figure out how you can help your partner with whatever they need. Even if you're the problem, listen and hear them out. Take the time to learn something new about yourself that you might not have noticed if your spouse didn't tell you. The goal is to gain an understanding of you and your partner. The greatest reflection of myself doesn't come from a mirror; it comes from my spouse. Sometimes we can go blind to our own dysfunctions, and it took me trusting my reflection (my spouse) to start seeing myself in a different light.

Learn me while I learn you, and we'll become one.

Oneness can only happen through love and communication, so talk to your partner, and aim to gain a solid understanding. If your partner understands how you feel, it will help them understand how to treat you.

You are not going to lose yourself by letting your spouse in.

This does not mean that your spouse becomes a slave to your feelings. Let down your guard, get rid of your pride, and accept that healthy communication leads to healthy love. It means your partner will have a better understanding of what you do and why you do it.

I am a communicator. When my spouse tells me everything on her mind, it never feels boring or old to me. The more, the better, and I'm grateful when she puts me in a position to win in our relationship by knowing her. The more she communicates about what I need to know to love her better, I feel strongly about the consistent, upward direction of our relationship.

Communication is key to any relationship, period. The following are scriptures about love and communication: Proverbs 12:8, Proverbs 15:1, Colossians 4:6. Pray over these verses in your spare time.

"Be completely humble and gentle; be patient, bearing with one another in love."

(Ephesians 4:2)

3

Partnership

Partnerships are common, but having a healthy partnership is special.

To have a person with the same relationship goals is awesome as if you have the cheat code to a happily ever after. Imagine having a common goal with your partner.

What if your goal is for no one to lack in the relationship, emotionally, spiritually, and mentally?

What if you and your partner told each other everything?

What if your partner woke up thinking about how to make your day better and vice versa?

What if your goal is to support whatever it is that the other wanted to do?

What if both parties believed and acted on equality in a relationship?

What if both parties understood that no one is perfect, and grace and forgiveness are keys to a lasting partnership?

Teamwork makes a dream work, so work as a team!

Imagine if you and four of your closest friends were challenged to a game of five on five, and when you show up to play, you find out that the other team only wants to use two of their five people to play. Even though the other three players are more than willing to help, the two remaining opponents want to do everything themselves. Well, who do you think will win? Certainly, the team of five.

Similarly, in a relationship, when one person does their own thing and chooses against being on the same accord with their partner, they're essentially forfeiting their chance to succeed. How could one expect to win or even compete without holding their partner to the highest regard? Integrity plays a huge role in a partnership. If you agree to do something, do it, or gracefully bow out and admit you changed your mind.

Respect your partner.

Be true to your word.

Listen to your partner's feelings.

Combine your thoughts with their thoughts, ideas, perceptions, and imperfections, without attempting to control or manipulate your partner. Exercising healthy communication does not mean you must agree on everything. A person of integrity seeks to communicate better, to be a part of something, not apart – not to be confused with wanting separation.

A part of – a partnership with someone is a joint effort.

Do it together. Build together with one common goal – one heart, one mind, one soul, and one flesh. Together. A partnership. A part of something.

You play your part, and I'll play my part, and together, we will be a part of something built by two people trying to achieve one thing and that's togetherness forever.

If you love your partner and want to spend the rest of your life with your partner, participate in your partner's wants and desires. Support them on their journey and make it your journey. Uncover the best qualities about your partner and try to implement those into your life to make yourself a better person and encourage them to do the same for you. Each one, teach one, and grow together.

God was intentional when He made marriage. I think He created marriage for us to not only have someone to spend the rest of our lives with but as a daily inspiration for the qualities that partners see in one another.

Look at your relationship with Christ. We are in a relationship to become more like Him, right? So, as we become one in our partnership, let's also mirror Christ.

A partnership needs honesty.

A partnership needs trust.

A partnership needs commitment.

Honesty, trust, and commitment – the foundation on which a solid partnership is built – and love is the key to open the door. Love will help you forgive and forget. Everyone needs grace and forgiveness. Everyone falls short of His glory. No one is perfect, only God. He is the only perfect partner.

As you and your partner reveal your feelings and thoughts to one another, you must accept that some of those admissions may be difficult to swallow. Perhaps your past decisions and journey include unfavorable truths. Well, that's to be expected. We are flawed human beings, and sin is a part of human nature. Our world is fallen, and no one is exempt from sinning: "Watch and pray that you may not enter into temptation. The spirit indeed is willing, but the flesh is weak" (Matthew 26:41). Keeping this in mind, you must commit to protecting your partner's feelings by not punishing them for what they've trusted you to know.

A solid partner never takes their partner's admissions and uses them to manipulate.

A solid partner never takes their partner's sensitive information and uses it for their advantage.

A solid partner never takes their partner's past and uses it in an augment to hurt their partner's feelings.

A solid partner never takes their partner's kindness for weakness.

A solid partner never gossips about their partner.

Have you ever used what your partner told you as ammunition to give you the upper hand, or did you use this information as a basis for repair and healing?

One of the many reasons people fall in love and stay in love is because they found a person who makes them feel safe, loved, and understood. Imagine sharing your innermost feelings with your partner, only to have those same feelings used as toxic collateral in the future.

Well, I doubt that would be well-received, and I can guarantee you will find yourself alone if you live by those standards.

No one likes to look stupid or foolish.

No one likes to be taken advantage of.

No one deserves to be treated poorly.

If you're not trying to build something honest and lasting with your partner, reconsider your motives and how you spend your time with that person. When you try to deceive your partner, things go wrong. To use a person's feelings to your advantage is wrong. Love your partner how they want to be loved, and if you are incapable of that, that relationship is not for you or need some time to be solo and reflect. Unfortunately, good intentions and deception often go hand in hand, yet people don't realize that at the moment.

In a partnership, it's easier to do things the right way the first time around. You can risk having the chance to fix something you've messed up, but why fix it when you don't have to do it the wrong way? Doing things the right way isn't losing or giving your partner their way. Your partner is trying to get you to see that your partnership will survive if you do things the right way on purpose. God saw fit to put your spouse in your life to help each other be great. Where you are weak, they are strong, and where they lack, you thrive. One of the best parts about having someone special is that you don't have to face anything alone.

A life partner is nothing to rush or not take seriously. A life partner is a serious commitment. If you choose to have a family, this will be the person who will help raise your children. This will be the person you date, the person you pray with, and the person you trust. After your long days at work, this is the person you come home to, the person who feels like home no matter where you are. So, take your time choosing your partner. Pray about your partner. Be aggressive about pursuing happiness for your future. For those in a partnership, cherish your spouse. Never forget to date your spouse. Don't stop communicating, either. A partnership is a long journey between two people, and ultimately, the goal is to become one.

"Enjoy life with the wife whom you love, all the days of your vain life that he has given you under the sun, because that is your portion in life and in your toil at which you toil under the sun."

(Ecclesiastes 9:9)

4

The House or the Ring

If the father of the bride is paying for or paid for the wedding, skip this chapter, but if the groom and the bride are saving for their wedding, please continue to read. Also, if you have the money to spend on a wedding, big or small, this chapter does not pertain to you, either. Truth be told, this chapter is for people who don't have a lot of money for a wedding.

Nuptial finances aren't exactly cut and dry for every relationship. Each situation is different, but here are a few questions to consider on this rather touchy topic:

Will the groom and bride pay for each other's rings?

Will that cost be split down the middle?

If either person already has kids or if the couple has children together, how will these responsibilities affect their wedding-based decisions?

I don't think anything is wrong with an expensive wedding ring but is life better because of a big engagement ring, an expensive wedding dress, or a huge wedding ceremony? What if you don't have a bachelor or bachelorette party? Does that mean you won't have a good marriage or a good life?

If your marriage expenses cost five figures, but you live in an apartment, your priorities are off.

A wedding lasts two hours.

A honeymoon lasts about one week.

Your future with your spouse is forever.

Why not invest in your future, such as buying a house to live in comfortably, purchasing a reliable vehicle, or pursuing a business venture?

I don't have anything against weddings. In fact, I love celebrations of love. My wife and I had a modest wedding of about 50 guests. We loved every minute of it, and although our wedding was on the smaller side in terms of guests, we know that other people may not envision those circumstances for their big day.

God created marriage, and that's precisely why I don't speak against weddings. They're acts of God. However, I'm merely stating that there is a right way and a wrong way to do things from a financial standpoint, yet people allow the culture to dictate the outcome of their lives more than their common sense and the Holy Spirit. People put more pressure on themselves than needed. "Keeping up with the Joneses" is real. No one wants to look like they don't have what their peers have, so most people go into debt and live above their means to keep up with others. Taking this approach causes problems in one's marriage, and you start your marriage off with a financial burden which can become a source of contention down the road.

Prior to discussing wedding finances, ask yourself the following:

Are you getting married to look good for your peers?

Are you getting married because you're in love with your partner?

Is deciding to spend the rest of your lives together the right thing to do?

I can tell you what the wrong thing would be – spending your hard-earned money on a ring and a wedding yet living in your mom's basement. Life happens, and that may cause you to be down on your luck, propelling you to move in with family, but that's different than willingly putting yourself in that position. Spending your money on a wedding and a ring are two ways to fall on your luck and be broke. When a man seems reluctant to get married, he often believes he is not financially ready. A man wants to be financially stable so he can take care of his family. Everything in life should be led with purpose. With that said, would you want to go into bankruptcy on purpose? Do you want to live paycheck to paycheck after you get married? Of course not! Wouldn't you rather have thousands saved before you get married instead of spending it on a ceremony that's going to last a few hours? One would think that a person would not want to live in poverty.

Prioritize your life and well-being.

Do things the right way.

Would you encourage your child to marry someone who only saved enough money to get married but wouldn't be able to care for a family, let alone their partner? If so, those parents might as well get the basement ready for their kids. You can get married without spending a great deal of money. How much you spend should depend on how much money you saved. If you are not financially stable, opt for a small wedding and make it special by adding thoughtful, outward expressions of love or creating a tradition. Invite the special people who love you. Focus on buying a house and securing a means of transportation. Remember – when and if you want to have the wedding of your dreams, have it on a significant anniversary when you can afford to spend. Why not have a small wedding and, hopefully, God blesses your finances so that in ten to 20 years, you can have a big celebration?

Yes to marriage.

No to going into debt because of a wedding ceremony.

Keep in mind – the first ring does not have to be the last ring. If you can afford the big diamond, by all means! If you can't, purchase what you can afford without breaking the bank. It's about how much you love one another, not the size of the diamond. Are you in love with your future spouse, or are you in love with the idea of marriage?

I understand why people like nice things. Hell, I like nice things, but I refuse to go broke to keep up with others. A married couple is to exchange rings during the ceremony, but the size of the ring is not specified anywhere. Preference is relative. Do not try to live up to the hype of marriage in terms of material possessions. Live up to the hype of love and doing things the right way in a marriage. Each couple knows what's best for their marriage and lifestyle. The fact of this matter is wasting money on a ceremony is not the best way to start a marriage. Be wise and prepare accordingly.

Don't follow the trends.

Follow your heart.

Your family is too valuable to make a poor, costly decision, a decision about money that can affect your household for a long time and set you back. Break the cycle of societal pressure. Do what pleases you and your spouse and don't succumb to the hype. Do you know how many people leave this earth with nothing to give their children because they wanted to live up to what everybody around them was doing instead of doing what they knew was right?

Make wise decisions.

Make sense of your life.

Put everything in order.

Prepare for your future children.

Start your marriage off right by putting you and your spouse in a position to win.

"Therefore, preparing your minds for action, and being sober-minded, set your hope fully on the grace that will be brought to you at the revelation of Jesus Christ. As obedient children, do not be conformed to the passions of your former ignorance but as he who called you is holy, you also be holy in all your conduct."

(1 Peter 1:13-15)

5

Who Cares?

Who cares who makes the most money in a relationship?

Well, some people certainly care, but this topic is wildly outdated and needs put to rest, especially as we strive for equality. All that really matters is who understands money matters. In other words, who effectively handles money? Who can save money, invest, and pay bills on time? Within your relationship, those are valuable questions to raise, and the answers to those questions should point to this conclusion – the person with financial knowledge should handle the money and educate their partner, so that money matters are widely understood within the partnership. Opting to have one person handle the money does not make the other partner weak. It's merely delegating proper responsibility. When each spouse is well-versed on money matters, a happy house is inevitable. Truth be told, most of the relationship problems I've counseled friends about were regarding financial issues. Couples find a way to move past emotion-centered problems, but financial issues birth an entirely different monster. So, this topic is certainly worth examining.

If a man and woman start their marriage and careers making $35,000 a year, but as time progresses, the woman ends up making significantly more than her husband, is it wrong for the wife to ask her husband to stay home and manage the household? At this point, they also have kids, so he would be responsible for helping with their homework and projects. Sure, he could start a business from home and make extra money, but does his stay-at-home status make him a no-good lazy husband or does this couple prioritize based on strengths?

Imagine meeting this couple for the first time, asking them what they do for a living, and they tell you that she works and he stays home. Would you automatically think that's wrong and the husband should carry his own weight? What if your daughter told you that she was going to work and her fiancé was going to stay home and take care of the kids? Would you castigate their decision based on traditional gender roles? People need to stop following trends and stop trying to keep up with the culture. Instead, we must use wisdom in every decision. It doesn't matter who is going to work. It only matters that each person is doing their task the right way, whether at home or at work.

Do not think less of yourself for letting your partner handle certain things in your marriage. Love the life you live and be confident in your decisions together.

Yes, paying bills on time is important for your marriage and credit scores. Your lifestyle depends on bills, credit, and timely payments. Your child's upbringing is important, too, and so is your spiritual journey and family's safety. Everything works together. At-home responsibilities do not define a person's worth, nor does that mean the person who stays home is lazy or less important. That's foolish! Remember to do more of what makes you happy while taking care of your responsibilities. Know your place and own it to keep the marriage going. Regarding the well-being of yourself, your spouse, and your kids, go the extra mile – it's never crowded. You'll feel better about yourself knowing that you did all that you could to have the best marriage and home life.

Yes, finances are important.

Yes, paying your bills on time is important.

Yes, making good money to take care of your family is important.

Yes, your credit score is important.

That's why whoever is better at those matters of importance needs to take the lead and give their family the best life they deserve. It does not matter if certain tasks are known to be a man's job or a woman's responsibility. It just needs to be done the right way and on time. Handle your responsibilities, no matter how big or small. If your ego gets in the way, you better believe the entire house will feel its effects.

God said man shouldn't be alone (Genesis 2:18), but God didn't say who should pay the bills. Communicate with your spouse and determine who's better at what. Then, execute a plan. Lean on one another's strengths and be aware of one another's weaknesses.

There's no one way of doing things, but there is a right and wrong way for your family. For example – if you and your spouse are saving money, and you had talked about what you wanted to do with the money, how disrespectful would it be for you to take that money and spend it on yourself on top of not communicating with your spouse about those plans? As awful as that sounds, situations like that happen all the time in marriage. That's why communicating about strengths and weaknesses is vital. That is why seeking balance is much needed, especially regarding finances. My wife helped me learn how to get more bang for my buck. In return, I helped my wife with saving some of the money we make. We pinpointed our financial strengths and shared those with each other. We are better for it, too.

Are your decisions financially helping or hurting your family?

Do you care about your family being successful?

Do you want your children to have to pay their way through college?

Do you want to position your children to win?

Are you well-versed in matters of finance?

Are you knowledgeable about retirement accounts, savings accounts, and stocks?

The answers to those questions will help you and your partner decide who to handle the finances. All you must do is swallow your pride, humble yourself, and allow God's grace to work in your life.

You may be wondering, "How is grace tied to finances?"

Well, God puts a person in your life that is good at something, something that may be a personal weakness, and you must recognize that this is for your benefit. God sent you a helpmate, so having someone to help you with your financial problem is actually a blessing if you allow God to work in your life. Everyone in your family loses when you make poor financial decisions, but when you know better, you can do better. Wisdom will tell you to follow the lead of your spouse who is better equipped at handling financial situations. I can't stress enough that everyone is not good at everything. You might be good at making money but keeping money and doing the right thing with money are entirely different things. If you prefer to handle the family's finances, educate yourself and learn how to conduct yourself with money. Your life will be more carefree because you and your partner will have established your weaknesses and strengths. If you ask me, there's nothing to be upset about regarding a transparent conversation about money. Throw out the cultural ideals that money management is gender related. Instead, responsibly enjoy the fruits of your labor and be sure to thank one another for their role within your partnership. It's never about who's doing it, as long as it's getting done. Where God guides, He provides (Isaiah 58:11).

"The Lord will guide you always; he will satisfy your needs in a sun-scorched land and will strengthen your frame. You will be like a well-watered garden, like a spring whose water never fail."

(Isaiah 58:11)

6

Don't Change After the Ring

No one wants to look or feel like a fool.

No one wants to look like they've been played.

No one wants to receive the short end of the stick.

Those are lonely places to start a new life with your partner. Not getting what you originally signed up for is a devastating experience. Yes, everyone is allowed to change and should evolve, but digressing is not part of the plan, especially not after someone says, "I do."

Imagine your fiancé cooks a delicious meal every Friday, but after you get married, he never touches another pot again, claiming he hates cooking. You, his wife, are now disappointed because you thought this was one of his hobbies, a hobby you enjoyed, too, as these Friday night meals made you feel extra special.

That's manipulation.

Perhaps he wasn't manipulating, though, but when he pumped the brakes on cooking, it showed an element of carelessness.

You shouldn't do something you know a person likes, such as cooking, to get something you want, such as marriage. That's not fair, and every relationship needs to be built off truth, trust, and honesty. The foundation needs to be strong so it can withstand the tests of time. Selling someone something broken is a crime and creates false, one-sided hope, the same way one person in the relationship knows they're being dishonest yet commits to those lies to keep their partner. How big or small the matter is irrelevant. If a man always wanted to marry a woman who shared his passion for sports, and based on her enthusiasm for sporting events, believed they shared this commonality… but now that they're married, she reveals she is bored by sports, is that a small or big deal? How would you feel?

Do not present the best version of yourself to someone when you first meet them if you're not prepared to commit to being that person in the long run. That's a false version of yourself that you can't keep going even if you wanted. Could it be that you believe the real you isn't good enough to keep someone happy in a relationship, so you lie to keep a person interested in you? Do you mask your identity to cover your insecurities? At the beginning of a relationship, what reasons do you withhold your genuine self? Examine your reasons for knowingly deceiving another person. When that person falls in love with a false version of you, then marries you only to discover the real version of you, is your partner expected to deal with it? No one deserves to be treated that way.

Do not deceive others.

Do not lie to get what you want.

Keep it real from the beginning.

Allow your partner to make a choice to be with the real you.

In a perfect world, everyone would be honest when they first meet people, and this honesty would continue until the day we die. If you didn't realize you've changed and it's been brought to your attention – and I'm not referring to growth or elevation – act accordingly, acknowledge it, consider your partner's feelings, and don't make light of it or be dismissive.

Being bamboozled isn't love and being led astray isn't moral.

When you lie, you're not thinking about your partner – you're only thinking of yourself and what works best for you when you should be thinking about your partnership and how to make things work best for both parties.

Selfishness will ruin your marriage.

Wanting to always win will ruin your marriage.

Never wanting to be wrong will ruin your marriage, but acknowledging your mistakes is the beginning of fixing yourself. First, you must acknowledge the mistake. Then, you must learn from your mistake. There are no losses in life, only lessons. The only "L" you take is the lesson. Don't be so stubborn that you don't want to change for yourself, improve your marriage, and show appreciation for the person you love. You only get one life. Make it a good one. Don't change after the ring for the sake of the ring. Chase after the love for the sake of a healthy, life-long partnership.

Love yourself and make decisions that reflect self-care. When you love yourself, you also give your partner the best version of the person they married. Aim to create a new goal for yourself every year. Yes, you're allowed to change. In fact, you should change! Just make changes for the better – a better marriage, a better lifestyle, a better bank account, and a better person. Keep loving yourself, and that will also help you better love your spouse.

Don't only do what makes you feel better. Consider your spouse. You're married and must move with your partner in mind. Involve your spouse in your decisions. Do not pretend to be something for someone knowing that you're going to change after you get what you want.

Being misled hurts, and deception feels terrible.

Communicate changes you're making to improve.

Changing for the better is awesome.

Grow and blossom into your true self; just bring your spouse on the journey with you. Your spouse doesn't have to participate in your growth, but they deserve to know where you're at in life because the goal is to remain one. Certain physical changes will happen that you can't avoid such as hair loss or wrinkles, but the changes I'm referring to are regarding deceit. Think about it this way – imagine building a custom home, and the builders ask for all types of information so that you get exactly what you want. After months of construction and the builders assuring you that the process is going wonderfully, the home is finally finished, but when you move in, the layout and details are different than what you requested. The oak floors you requested are tile, the walk-in-closets are nowhere to be found, and the kitchen has an electric oven opposed to gas. How would that make you feel? Understandably, you would be furious, especially considering the lengthy, ongoing communication between you and the builders. Well, in a relationship, when someone tricks another person into marrying them on the belief that they are one way and it turns out that they are a completely different person, they feel indescribably heartbroken and confused.

I urge you to check yourself.

Do a self-evaluation to assess whether your identity is on par with your true self and the person your partner married.

Before I got married, I made some changes for the better. I gave my life to Jesus Christ. As my faith grew, I realized God was molding me into a better man – a man with stronger morals, a man with solid values, and a man who held the utmost respect for his loved ones. These changes made me a better partner.

Folks, let's not change for the worst after getting married.

No one wants or deserves the short end of the stick.

Don't play with someone's heart like that.

Be an honest person and remain the person your spouse married.

Don't change after the ring.

"Let your eyes look straight ahead; fix your gaze directly before you. Give careful thought to the paths for your feet and be steadfast in all your ways. Do not turn to the right or the left; keep your foot from evil."

(Proverbs 4:25-27)

7

Your Partner is Not a Sex Slave

Everything should be communicated at the beginning of a relationship, including preferences about sex and affection. If sex is all you want, rather than having a monogamous relationship, tell your partner to avoid misleading them. If you like having sex every day, tell your partner and be sure to respect their preference, too. Whatever your preference, whether every day or not as frequent, it's important to tell the truth about how you really feel about sex.

Listen, sex is an important part of marriage. To avoid this topic is to negate an integral part of your relationship.

It's not perverted to discuss sex before marriage. Not telling someone how you feel is doing you and them a disservice. Everyone's appetite for intimacy is different. Some people enjoy converting to what their partner likes, whereas others are comfortable with their initial preference.

Should married people try new things?

Sure!

You never want the relationship to become stale. However, your partner is not a sex slave. There is a big difference between spicing things up and demanding your partner do things for the sake of your sexual appetite. Your partner does not have an obligation to do the things you heard in the breakroom at work. Asking your partner how they feel about trying new things, sexually speaking, is one thing but trying to force your partner or make them feel guilty for not doing it is wrong. Sex should be something both parties want. Be sure to communicate. After all, it will start to feel weird for the one who wants it all the time because they didn't initially communicate wants and needs prior to diving into the sex part of the relationship. If that's the case, the other spouse will start to feel like their partner doesn't want them sexually. After a while, you begin to feel unwanted.

Is it wrong for wanting to feel wanted by your spouse?

Absolutely not.

Fellas and ladies, be sure to understand the difference between fantasy and reality. A fantasy is just that – something you dream about doing. It doesn't have to be played out outside of your mind. It's a want and desire, but it's not a need.

If you tell your partner "no" because you're tired or not in the mood, can you be jealous if they pleasure themselves in other ways? Do you only want to have sex when you're in the mood? If so, that's not a fair marriage or relationship. Fairness involves give and take. You shouldn't have one without the other. Yes, a person should at least try to get you in the mood, but your partner can't read your mind either. Communication is key, and because sex is a vital part of a relationship, you must talk about your needs and listen with an open heart.

Truth be told, I had to learn how to communicate with my spouse. I didn't get this until I was already married. So, I understand how you may feel because I've been there, done that. However, I've learned to appreciate my partner's time, boundaries, needs, and expectations. I understand that I can't expect anything from my partner unless I communicate with them.

There should be no expectations without communication.

Sure, sporadic and spontaneous sex is great, and everyone has a moment when they want something out of the blue. You should be free in your marriage to feel free, but there are also boundaries you shouldn't cross. For example – if your spouse had to be up late to finish work and needed to wake up early for work the next day, then it's not wise or considerate to pursue a spontaneous moment during that time. There is such a thing as perfect timing. If the time is right and the mood is right, go for it. Shoot your shot, just don't be mad if your shot gets blocked.

Consider your partner, and it goes without saying that this advice not only applies to sex. You should ensure everything is going well with the house and kids so your spouse can properly execute their task at hand. Maybe you can make them breakfast in bed or encourage a relaxing break by making your partner a cup of coffee. Maybe you can iron or steam their outfit or make sure your spouse has gas in their car. Whatever it is, do it with love and expect nothing in return for loving your spouse.

Understanding your partner's appetite is important. Remain in the know and support their desires while respecting your boundaries. Give your situation a chance to reach a place of understanding through conversation. Maybe you can convince them to see things your way, as long as you're not trying to deceive or hurt the other person. Please, whatever you do, don't use cheating with someone else as an excuse to do different things. Don't say your spouse isn't willing to listen, compromise, or try new things because you're the one afraid to ask and communicate. A closed mouth can't get fed. In terms of sex, remain committed to being a loving partner who loves to satisfy and please their spouse. Love your partner and support their wants while supporting your desires, too.

Remember – when someone feels genuinely loved and cared for, they are more likely to want to return that love, too. Having a great partner means being a great partner.

In the first chapter of the book, the topic of a two-way street is touched on regarding men not communicating with their wives and speaking negatively about their marriage with other married men, family, and friends. Circling back to this important notion – men and women need to discuss why they go out and find a partner that satisfies them in ways outside of their spouse. Cheating is rooted in selfishness and miscommunication. When needs aren't met, communication must ensue.

Some men wonder how to properly explain to their wife exactly what they want without their wants coming off strangely.

Some women wonder how to ask their men to do certain things in bed without raising red flags.

Generally, people want to feel wanted and needed. Knowing someone is attracted to you brings a different feeling to the relationship. That's why it's easier to cheat because the new person seems into you and expresses how much they want you. Judgment becomes clouded and people willingly receive what's been chasing them. It's been said that women cheat for emotional reasons and men cheat for the physical aspect. This can't be said for every situation, of course, but the truth is, women are more commonly pursued, wooed, and spoiled with affection and gestures. Women don't often walk up to men and ask them out on a date. For the most part, men are not used to being approached in a sexual manner by a woman. Nevertheless, men want to feel wanted, too. A man wants to feel attractive. A man wants to know when you like the cologne he's wearing. Ladies, a man wants his spouse to want him sexually.

Compromise is needed in a marriage to equally exchange thoughts on two different minds with different sexual appetites. Becoming one in a marriage, including the aspect of sex, will take time, but the main goal is to understand what makes your partner tick.

Serious question – let's say your oldest child in their late 20s comes home one day and tells you that their partner is adamant about them doing a specific sexual act a few times a day, but your child isn't feeling this. How would you feel about that? How would you respond? Would you want someone to look at your child as a sex object? I highly doubt it. I share that to share this – view everyone from God's eyes. If you're looking at a woman, view her as God's daughter and treat her as such. If you are looking at a man, view him as God's son, and treat him as such.

Forcing yourself on someone is morally, legally, emotionally, and physically wrong. Please respect everyone and their decisions. No one wants to be used and abused by someone they love. No one wants to feel like someone's sex slave. Communicate and be upfront with your spouse. Tell them how you feel about sex before you get married. Allow your partner the opportunity to decline your invitation if they're not interested.

With a patient spirit, communication, and selflessness, anything is possible in a marriage, including an amazing sex life.

"The heart of her husband trusts in her, and he will have no lack of gain."

(Proverbs 31:11)

8

Your Partner is Not Your Bank

Finances.

Here we go again.

Trust me, we need to harp on this topic because it's deeper than budgeting and saving.

Some people look for their spouse to financially take care of them while they sit back and do nothing. Some people look for wealthy or hard-working people to marry so they won't have to work hard themselves. Looking for someone to take care of them for the rest of their life and not pitching in is unfair and wrong. If a man or woman meets someone and that person wants to take care of them, that is a completely different situation, and I am all for that because the standards and expectations are communicated and shared.

There is nothing wrong with someone financially taking care of someone else.

There is something wrong, however, with someone trying to manipulate someone else to spend their money on them knowing that they don't love them or want to do nice things in return.

If you are not the breadwinner for your household, be the best at whatever it is that you do for your family. That is not a lessor job for you or your family. Couples come in all shapes and sizes, meaning – each relationship is different, and that includes the financial aspect. Whether you're financially comfortable or working toward financial freedom, remember these key pieces of advice:

Live within your means.

Love your spouse.

Set goals for your life.

Celebrate milestones, big and small.

Pursue your dreams.

Remember – do not attempt to live through others. Jealousy breeds envy. Be a trendsetter. Make what you're doing cool. Be wise with your spending and don't disappoint your partner by spending your hard-earned money on a fad that won't be around this time next year.

Your bills will still be here.

Your children will still be here.

Your mortgage will still be here.

Your car note will still be here.

So, let's not forget about what's most important to you and your family. Make the right decisions the first time and refuse to put your family in the hole. If you want something and don't have enough money for it, talk to your spouse about it. Ask them to help you save for it. Make it a family mission. Do it as a family. Remember – your children watch your every move. It's okay to get it wrong in the beginning but show your children that you've learned and prepared to do it the right way the next time. Something you want to buy can be put on your birthday or holiday list. It might not be when you want it but at least you're still getting it – *the right way*.

Everyone grew up differently. Maybe you saw mom or dad spending money a certain way and thought it was right, but you eventually learned that their financial habits were toxic. Well, repeating those patterns is wrong and needs to change.

Why not have a real discussion about your finances instead of silently opening a separate bank account to make sure your life doesn't tumble by accident from a decision made by your spouse who's not good at handling money? If your spouse is making a conscious decision to put finances aside to upgrade your lifestyle, it would not be wise to do anything to sabotage the sacrifice. Money puts a major strain on a lot of relationships and ends a lot of marriages. One person in the marriage may feel like the other person is taking advantage of them and how they handle money. Other couples have the mentality of "what's mine is yours and what's yours is mine." Again, each relationship differs. Nevertheless, when you're married, you and your partner are in this thing called life, together. When one person in the marriage takes bumps and bruises, their spouse tends to feel those bruises as well. Upon agreeing to be in a marriage, you also agree to take care of your partner financially. Annihilate selfishness and become one with your spouse so that unintentional mishaps with spending money don't abruptly appear. Without balance and communication, you can nix a happy spouse and happy house. Worse, you'll be faced to examine the following questions:

If your spouse saved extra money after paying their bills, do you think that the money your spouse saved belongs to you?

Would you be mad if you found out that your spouse had a separate bank account and was saving money just in case something went wrong or saved it for a rainy day?

If you showed yourself to be financially irresponsible, is it wrong for your partner to cover themselves and protect their children?

Do you believe having a separate bank account is going too far?

Is talking about divorce and money in the same sentence going too far?

When should you or your partner be held accountable for financial mistakes?

Money is no laughing matter and not to be taken lightly. In fact, money is a genuine struggle for some folks, in which they need to pray about and talk to a therapist. Not only should you have honest conversations about money with your partner, but I encourage you to acknowledge your mistakes and mishandlings, too. Everyone takes time to do something they want. So, take the time and become a better person for yourself and your marriage. To be financially stable is good for you and your family, and to attain and maintain stability is a blessing.

Learn from your mistakes.

Put your past behind you.

Take your finances seriously.

Show your spouse your seriousness of the matter.

Show your children how much they mean to you by improving how you feel about your money, how you handle money, and how you teach them about money.

If properly handling money is hard for you to conquer, remember to leave your pride at the doorstep and talk to someone about this issue. When you know better, you do better. A lack of surrender shows a lack of love for yourself and your family. Think of this topic in terms of the military – when a person goes to the military, they are expected to focus on their military assignments because the safety and well-being of others depend on their actions. Well, in a marriage, you have several assignments, one of which is financial responsibility, and the safety and well-being of your marriage depend on this. A series of small commitments will change your life in a big way. Use wise counsel, seek a good support system, and remember to always try to do the right thing. You and your family depend on it.

"He that walketh uprightly walketh surely: but he that perverteth his ways shall be known."

(Proverbs 10:9)

9

Say "Yes." Then, Say "No."

The moment you accept your spouse's hand in marriage is when you should say "no" to everyone else.

Say "no" to everyone you've flirted with before.

Say "no" to the person who thinks they have a shot at taking you on a date.

Say "no" to the person who always offers to buy you lunch whenever you're in the lunchroom, and you know their motives are far from platonic.

It was cool before you got married, and those boundaries should've been established when you got engaged, but as a married person, you need to sever the temptation and inappropriate advances. It's also not respectful to talk about scandalous topics with certain people. Those conversations lead to confusion and blurred lines. Some of these situations may not seem clear at the moment but it's up to you to tap into your discernment. For example – prior to getting married, you went on a few dates with your coworker. Things didn't work out, but you remained cordial at the office. However, now that you're married, your coworker continues to steer conversations toward the topic of sex. Rather than engaging in these conversations, you shut them down. It would not be wise to behave in a manner that would leave a person confused and believing you're single or welcoming their advances. That's foolishness and your spouse does not deserve to be treated with disrespect. Those behaviors are unacceptable and misleading. Anything you don't speak against stretches boundaries and becomes permissible.

Do not be scared to protect your marriage.

Have the strength and morality to tell people you are not okay with their comments and actions.

Let people know that they made you feel uncomfortable.

Each couple's boundaries differ and establishing these is necessary so that you both know how one another feels regarding pressing topics.

Are you and your partner okay with accepting gifts from others?

Is it okay to accept favors from people?

Do you let it go because it helps you save money?

Ladies and gentlemen, we must be aware. People commonly want something from somebody. That's not to say that people always have an underlying motive because many people are genuinely kind; however, some people prey on other people's happiness.

Be aware.

Protect your peace.

Do not allow unnecessary drama to unfold in your marriage.

If you would never cheat or deceive your partner, know that stretching boundaries is planting seeds of deceit, even if your intentions are pure. Once a seed is planted, you don't know how it will blossom. For example – you've been harmlessly flirting with someone at the gym. One day, they notice you're upset. So, they walk to the weight room to check on you and discover you've had a heated fall out with your spouse. Some people use this opportunity to make a strong pass at you. Perhaps your anger or sadness clouded your judgment, and before you know it, you're in an affair with someone because the harmless flirting led to a physical relationship.

Don't be quick to talk badly to others about your spouse. After you make up with your spouse, the people you talked about them to may hold a grudge against your partner. Now, every time you have a disagreement, your friend or family will tell you to leave them because they never forgave them for the last thing you told them about your partner. Cover your spouse and keep the business of your marriage in your home. Everything is not for everybody. Just because you can't stand the sight of your spouse now does not mean you'll feel that way forever. When problems arise in your marriage, take it to God. Share your feelings and concerns. He is always listening. Also, opt for wise counsel. Choose friends that give sound, fair advice, advice that explores all perspectives. When choosing the right listeners, you will avoid unnecessary harm to your marriage.

I like to make sure that my friends know and love my wife. Some people like to keep their friends separate, and there is nothing wrong with that. Everyone is different, but I prefer to be the let's-hang-together husband. I cherish my friends and adore my wife, so it feels great to be together at once.

As we've grown in our marriage, I also recognize that I'm an affectionate, up-close-and-personal type of husband. Heck, I'll grease her scalp if she asks. My wife, on the other hand, feels recharged when given small tokens of appreciation or thoughtful gestures. Our love languages are different, yet we match well. Where I'm weak, she's strong and vice versa. Although we prefer different types of affection, we recognize that we want what's best for each other.

Becoming one with your spouse isn't easy, but you must pray for your spouse to withstand pressure from friends and family.

Never get complacent in your marriage.

Make the commitment to loving your spouse unconditionally.

Nothing should be too much or too hard to do for your spouse.

Only do things to your spouse that you want to be done to you. If you don't want your spouse to have a "work wife" or a "work husband," then you shouldn't either. Set the tone for your marriage. Let this be the test – *whatever you can't say or do in front of your spouse shouldn't be said or done when they're not around.* If you wait to say or do certain things when your spouse is not around, that's sneaky. A person only sneaks to do things when they're not supposed to do it. Why get married to go behind your partner's back and do something deceitful?

Grow up.

Don't marry someone if you're not ready to be faithful.

Marry someone you love to be around, who you think about when they're not around.

Marry someone who loves you.

Marry someone who will always treat you with love and respect.

Marriage is a bond created by God, not to be played with, taken lightly, or forsaken. None of us always do everything right. We're never going to be perfect, and we all have made or will make another mistake, but what do you do after you realize you're wrong and need to change?

If you value yourself and your partner, the answer is this: *Change.*

Get off your high horse, humble yourself, and change to become a better version of yourself. It was once said that what one man or woman won't do for you, another man or woman will. Well, as a committed partner, you need to throw that expression out of the window. That mind frame does not apply to you because you understand and value the principals of communication and love. If you don't like something about your partner, or something bothers you about your relationship, that doesn't justify you to look elsewhere. The flesh can be deceiving. In fact, our fleshy emotions can get the best of us at times. Whether we explode during an argument when we should have remained calm or we inch closer to the temptation of flirting with someone else, our flesh can lead us to make spiritually bankrupt decisions. Again, I urge you to check yourself. If you can't keep it real with yourself, how can you keep it real with your spouse? Identify temptations and train your flesh to steer clear of those pitfalls. In marriage, the goal is to be loving, receptive, and faithful, no exceptions.

"For which of you, desiring to build a tower, does not first sit down and count the cost, whether he has enough to complete it?"

(Luke 14:28)

10

Commitment

Loving your spouse and being committed to your spouse are two separate things. If you care about their feelings, you will not cheat on your partner. In fact, no one would ever commit adultery. No one would ever step outside of their marriage because loving their spouse would be reason enough to remain faithful. Clearly, that's not the case because adultery happens often.

There's a gap in the way couples feel about commitment. Commitment is an engagement or obligation that restricts freedom of actions, not to be confused with being committed to a cause or activity. Marital commitment involves loyalty and trust. To be completely committed to your spouse, you must become one with them and should want for your spouse what you want for yourself.

You don't want to be betrayed, do you?

You don't want to be lied to, do you?

You don't want to be taken advantage of, do you?

Treat your spouse how you want to be treated. Don't let anyone come between you and your spouse. Don't be more excited to do something for someone else before you want to do it for your spouse. When a woman walks down the aisle at her wedding, her father gives her to her spouse-to-be for him to look after her and take care of her. The father understands his responsibilities of being her mentor, protector, and friend are now imparted to her spouse. From that moment on, the couple builds a union that should be unbreakable, unmovable, and covered in love, for others to watch from the sidelines, knowing no one could penetrate their force field if they tried.

Yes, as a couple, there will be disagreements and misunderstandings. It's not easy becoming one flesh. Once the journey begins, life continues to be ever-changing, and it's up to each person in the marriage to do their part. If you're the one who needs to change to keep the peace in your household, do it; change and grow. In turn, your partner should be willing to change in other areas, if and when that time comes. As you continue to grow, learn, and fight for your love, you become one. You will lose parts of your old self that you don't need anymore, yet as you reflect, don't be overly excited about the good times and deeply depressed about the bad times. Enjoy the journey. Experience is the best teacher.

The point is – commit to loving your spouse.

Commit to honoring your spouse.

Commit to caring for your spouse.

Treasure the little things that define your marriage. Perhaps you and your partner have a tradition of going skating every third Thursday of the month. Although this may seem routine, view this as a special blessing within your relationship, as many people don't have these unique dates. Look forward to that day. Let your partner know you can't wait for your skating date. Maybe think about surprising your partner with something to accompany this date, perhaps a new outfit or laces for their skates. Form an amazing partnership through the culmination of kind, small gestures.

Marriage is not just a ceremony; it's a commitment to God and your spouse.

As a husband, I have fallen short. I've lived and learned. No one is perfect but God, and this insight is not to steer you into feel guilty for your past. Pick yourself up, dust yourself off, and try again. Don't remain stagnant. Today is a new opportunity to do the right thing for your marriage.

Commitment fights for love. Commit to loving your spouse after they offend you or made a mistake. It's human nature to only remember what happened to you and not what you did to someone. We tend to point the finger but fail to self-reflect. Commit to working on yourself as often as possible because a happy spouse makes a house. You and your partner are equally important. It's not just a happy wife that makes a happy life. Happiness on both ends is needed for commitment. Continue to keep the fire lit in your marriage, and as you keep your flame strong, don't fall victim to the social media trap, either.

Social media is a mirage. Social media is a highlight real – sharing people's favorite or best moments – which is a beautiful thing, but this also leads to jaded views on relationship expectations. Please do not compare your marriage to any other marriage you see online. You don't know what goes on behind closed doors. Of course, many couples are as happy as they appear to the public. Then again, we never know the trials they've endured or how they struggle. Love doesn't make decisions based on social media. Love evolves based on time spent, memories made, and lessons learned.

Make time for love in your relationship. Time is one of the most important things you can give someone. You can't get time back after you've used it or passed it up. It's a priceless gift. Spend quality time with your spouse. Becoming one with your spouse means sharing a deep understanding of each other. If you're going to be addicted to anything on this Earth besides God, make it your spouse, to the point that their presence, company, and conversation fills your cup. It's no one's responsibility but yours to make sure that your marriage works. If there's integrity in the marriage, the marriage should win.

When you are whole, and your spouse is whole, your marriage will be whole.

When you have peace, and your spouse has peace, your marriage will have peace.

You are teammates, not opponents. No one should try to win the conversation. Instead, both parties should try to gain clarity and understanding. The goal is not to prove your point. The goal is for both parties to arrive at an understanding by way of respect and love. There will be times when someone may have to bend a little more, and that's okay because give and take is vital. The only win should be the win for the couple, not the individual.

When I think about being married to the woman of my dreams, my wife, I think of being in a competition to out-nice my spouse. I see myself going above and beyond to ensure our relationship is at its best. I know and understand I must work on myself and be the best person I can be before I try to improve our union.

Love your spouse.

Command your mind, body, and soul to commit to your spouse.

Marriage is supposed to be forever.

Don't give up on your spouse.

Give them time to grow.

Men, don't marry a woman so she can replace your mom. She's not the person who must cook and clean up after you. Women, don't marry a man to replace your dad. He's not the person who must baby you. Marry someone because you can't live without them. Marry someone who makes life more joyous.

Commit to your commitment.

Honor your vows.

Love your spouse.

Learn your spouse.

Learn yourself.

Love yourself.

Your spouse should be able to trust, believe, and rely on you. You should be each other's support system, life partners, forever, growing as one. Commitment doesn't equal control. Do not try to control everything. Be with someone who you don't mind changing into, as their qualities will become part of you and yours a part of them.

"Dear friends, since God loved us, we also ought to love one another. No one has ever seen God; but if we love one another, God lives in us and his love is made complete in us."

(1 John 4:11-12)

11

Walk in Love

There's a common saying in society – "Happy wife, happy life" – and although I've heard this a time or two, this expression has yet to resonate in our union.

Believe me, seeing my wife happy is an incredible, indescribable feeling, yet during the course of our two-becomes-one journey, we've learned something far more valuable that has created an environment of respect, love, and honor within our marriage – "Happy spouse, happy house."

There are many toxic concepts that people equate to peace and happiness in a relationship, and they stem from a lack of equality. Giving a man sex in exchange for his time, love, or presents is not a fair exchange of emotion. Planning a lavish wedding, leaving little to start your life together, is irresponsible and leads to temporary happiness. Manipulation, leading to marriage, is deceitful, and pinning your spouse as anything other than a loving partner should not be their assumed role.

Your partner is not your sex slave.

Your partner is not your bank.

Your partner is not a possession.

When we know better, we do better, and when we commit to leaving our old ways behind to mature, humble ourselves, and grow, a relationship has room to flourish.

Pride is alive in many marriages, so is a refusal to change, a need to keep up and outdo other relationships, and a lack of personal responsibility. These prideful ways lead to disaster, specifically, divorce.

Let's break the cycle of divorce.

Let's appreciate one another.

Let's seek to be less selfish and more accommodating to our spouse.

Seek to climb the mountain of love to its highest height.

This metaphor, "climbing the mountain of love," is a way for me to describe my feelings about my marriage. I envision my wife at the very top, and nothing will stop me from climbing that mountain. I also understand that this is an uphill climb, and that isn't always easy. Climbing the mountain of love keeps me in the mind frame of working extremely hard for something I want, which happens to be love. Even though the climb is something I want to do, I understand its difficult, but ultimately, my spouse is worth the journey. On your climb, you might come face to face with unexpected problems, you might grow tired, and you may need to figure out a new path to climb, but you are all in, and you move to the top of the mountain with love, faith, and strength.

Go forth and continue to climb or, perhaps, you're just starting. Whatever the case may be, let's reach the top!

"Happy spouse, happy house!"

Made in the USA
Monee, IL
09 July 2020

36265453R00066